The Az

ROSEMARY REES

Heinemann

First published in Great Britain by
Heinemann Library
an imprint of Heinemann Publishers
(Oxford) Ltd
Halley Court, Jordan Hill, Oxford OX2 8EJ

OXFORD LONDON EDINBURGH MADRID
ATHENS BOLOGNA PARIS MELBOURNE
SYDNEY AUCKLAND SINGAPORE TOKYO
IBADAN NAIROBI HARARE GABORONE
PORTSMOUTH NH (USA)

98 97 96 95 94
10 9 8 7 6 5 4 3 2 1

**British Library Cataloguing in Publication
Data is available from the British Library
on request.**

ISBN 0 431 07800 9 (Hardback)
    0 431 07781 9 (Paperback)

Designed by Ron Kamen, Green Door
Design Ltd, Basingstoke

Printed in China

Photographic acknowledgements
The author and publishers wish to
acknowledge with thanks the following
photographic sources:

a = above b = below l = left r = right

Ferdinand Anton pp20; Bodleian Library
pp10*a*, 11, 13*b*, 14–17, 28, 30*a*, 36, 42, 43*b*,
45, 46, 48;

C M Dixon pp7*a*, 33*b*
E T Archive pp57;
Werner Forman Archive pp4, 5, 6*b*, 7*b*, 8*b*,
9, 10, 13, 18, 19, 20, 22, 23, 26, 27, 28, 29*b*,
31*a*, 32, 33*a*, 37, 39, 40, 47, 49, 53, 59*a*
Alan Hutchison Library pp34, 35*a*
Mexican Embassy p59*b*
Marion and Tony Morrison p44;
Nick Saunders/Barbara Heller Archive p6*a*
Salmer p54
Syndication International pp24, 30*b*, 52*a*,
53.

The publishers have made every effort to
trace the copyright holders, but if they
have inadvertently overlooked any, they
will be pleased to make the necessary
arrangement at the first opportunity.

Cover photograph © Bodleian Library

Note to the reader – In this book there are some words in the text which are printed in **bold** type. This shows that the word is lited in the glossary on page 62. The glossary gives a brief explanation of words which may be new to you.

Contents

Who were the Aztecs?

The Aztec people, led by their emperor Montezuma, ruled over a huge, rich empire. This empire was in the land which is now called Mexico. Their capital, Tenochtitlan, was one of the world's largest cities. In 1519 the Spanish attacked. They destroyed the Aztec Empire. They also destroyed a lot of evidence that would have told us how the Aztecs lived.

Before the Aztecs

Civilizations existed in Mexico long before the Aztec Empire. The Olmecs lived in Mexico from about 1300BC. They were skilled **sculptors** and artists.

A Mixtec earring
This gold earring was made by the Mixtec people. They were skilled at making gold jewellery.

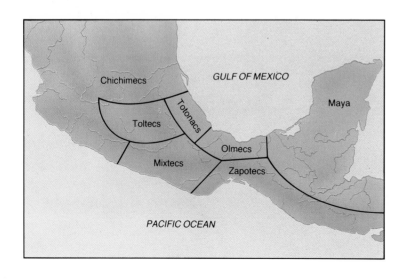

◀ This is a map of the land which is now modern Mexico. It shows where the people lived who were there before the Aztecs.

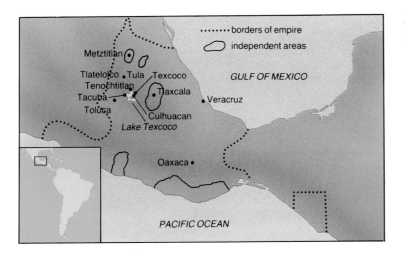

A map of the Aztec Empire in 1519

The Mayans lived in Mexico between AD300 and AD900. They were the first people in Mexico to use picture writing, or **glyphs**. The Toltecs settled in Mexico between AD900 and AD1150. Ruins of their buildings tell us they were great **architects**. When the Toltec empire collapsed, other tribes began to move into the area. The last tribe to arrive were the Aztecs.

At first the Aztecs had no land. In 1325 they settled on an island in the middle of Lake Texcoco. They built their capital city, Tenochtitlan, there. It became one of the biggest cities in the world. Within 200 years the Aztecs controlled an empire that stretched right across Mexico.

The Temple of the Warriors
This was built by the Toltecs. When the Aztecs built their temples, they copied some of the details from Toltec temples.

5

How do we know about the Aztecs?

We know about the Aztecs and how they lived because we can look at things from their time which still exist today. We can look at the ruins of their buildings. We can look at smaller things such as pottery and jewellery. We can look at the pictures they made. These **artefacts** (things made by people) are sometimes buried deep in the ground. **Archaeologists** are people who are specially trained to **excavate** and uncover ruins of buildings and towns. They dig carefully. They make drawings and take photographs of everything they uncover. They collect together everything they find. They use this evidence to explain how the Aztecs lived and what happened to them.

Templo Mayor in Mexico City
This temple stood in the square in the middle of Tenochtitlan. It was a temple to the gods Huitzilopochtli and Tlaloc. Archaeologists uncovered it.

The ruins of Teotihuacan
No one knows which tribe of people built this city in about 200BC. Archaeologists and historians think that the Aztecs copied the layout of Teotihuacan when they built Tenochtitlan.

Archaeology in Mexico

The Aztecs lived in a country which is now called Mexico. Mexico City is the capital of Mexico. It was built on top of the ruins of an Aztec city called Tenochtitlan. A few years ago, a new underground station was being built in Mexico City. As the builders dug deep into the ground, they discovered old ruins. They called in archaeologists, who said that the ruins had once been an Aztec temple. It was the temple of the Aztec God of the Wind, Ehecatl-Quetzalcoat.

Archaeologists excavated cities that were lived in long before the time of the Aztecs. They found artefacts that were very like Aztec artefacts. This tells us that the Aztecs used some of the ideas of earlier tribes.

Aztec pottery
The top picture is of a child's rattle.
The bottom picture is of small pottery stamps. They were dipped in paint and used to print patterns on Aztecs' faces.

History in pictures and words

Aztec writing

When the Aztecs wanted to write something they used little pictures, not words. These pictures are called glyphs. Each glyph was always drawn in the same way so everyone knew what the writer wanted to say. A footprint meant travel. A scroll meant speech. A shield and arrows meant war. Important people were drawn larger than people who were less important. Aztec **scribes** painted glyphs onto a kind of paper called **amatl**. The pages were joined together in a long zig-zag.

An Aztec book is called a **codex**. These codices tell us about Aztec history, prayers, calendars, taxes and farming.

Aztec glyphs
This glyph shows the Fire Serpent marrying a flower. It means 'the wind'.

A codex
An Aztec book is called a codex. The plural of codex is codices.

Spanish writers

In 1519 Spanish soldiers, led by Hernan Cortes, invaded Mexico and defeated the Aztecs. People from Spain went to live in Mexico. Spanish priests taught the Aztecs about Christianity. Some priests tried to find out more about the Aztecs and their way of life.

Father Bernadino de Sahagun arrived in Mexico in 1529. He learned the Aztec language, *Nahuatl*, and talked to the Aztec leaders. Later he wrote a book called *General History of the Things in New Spain*. He wrote it in Spanish and Nahuatl. Friar Diego Duran was another Spanish priest. He wrote three books about Aztec history.

The problem with histories of the Aztecs is knowing what to believe. A lot of what the Aztecs wrote about their own history was based on **legends** and so is not absolutely true. Spanish writers tried to show that the Aztecs were barbarians, and this is not really true either. It is important to remember who was writing and where their information came from.

A statue of the god Quetzalcoatl
The god is carrying a load of grain on his back. A long strap goes round his forehead. This gives us an idea about how the Aztecs carried loads.

9

Aztec government

The Aztecs were ruled by kings. When a king died, the **nobles**, **priests** and **warriors** chose a new one. The new ruler was always from the same family as the dead king. Aztec kings had to keep tight control over their **empire**. There were often wars and so the king had to be a good soldier.

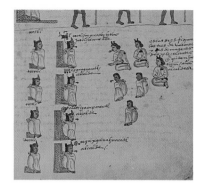

Crime and punishment
This picture from a codex shows an Aztec trial. The six people on the right are asking for justice from the judges on the left.
An Aztec punishment might be piercing the guilty prisoner with cactus spines or taking away his lands. Thieves were stoned or sometimes hanged. Prisoners could appeal to the Woman Snake or the Emperor if they did not agree with their punishment.

The headdress of Montezuma
The emperor Montezuma wore this headdress. It was made from precious stones and feathers from the quetzal bird.

After the king, the most important person was a man called the Woman Snake. He was in charge of law and order and collecting the taxes. There was a small **council** of four nobles, who gave the king advice. There was a larger council called the **tlatocan** which included tax collectors, judges and scribes. They discussed things such as the laws and whether they should be changed, and how much tax everyone should pay.

The calpulli family group

Every Aztec was a member of a **calpulli**. This was a clan or group of families who were related to each other. Calpullis organized the towns and villages where they lived. The calpullis owned the land, but were under the strict control of the king and the nobles. Each calpulli had a head man called a **calpullec.** His job was to see that the land was farmed properly and that **tributes** were paid on time. He had to make sure that the calpulli provided enough workers for the nobles. The nobles became more and more powerful after the 1420s, as the Aztec Empire grew larger.

A tribute list
The Aztecs made people they conquered pay tribute to them. This is a list of the tribute which had to be paid by 22 towns in the Tochtepec area. They had to send this amount of tribute to the Aztecs every year. Try to work out what they had to send.

What were Aztecs' clothes like?

The Aztecs thought it was important to know whether a person's position in society was high or low. People's rank showed in the way they dressed. There were three main groups in Aztec society: the nobles, the **commoners** and the **slaves**. Commoners were ordinary people, such as farmers and craft workers. Slaves were people who were too poor to pay their tributes or live off the land.

The rules of dress

Only the nobles were allowed to wear brightly coloured cloaks made from **cotton**, and sandals in the city. Commoners had to wear rough cloth. They were not allowed to wear anything which came below their knees.

Aztec clothes
The man on the right is a nobleman. We know this because he wears a cloak coming to below his knees and has sandals on his feet. Do you think the woman is from a noble family or not?

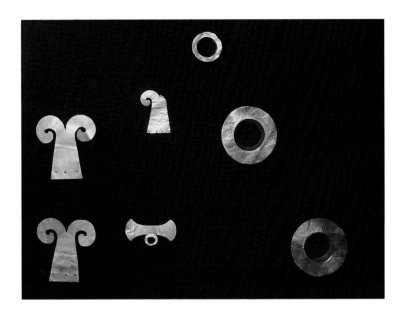

Gold nose and ear plugs
Aztec men and women wore these. They pierced their ears and their noses.

The Aztecs grew cotton and **maguey** plants and spun their fibres into thread. Every Aztec woman could weave the thread into cloth. They dyed the cloth with natural dyes made from flowers, vegetables, shellfish and insects. Most Aztec clothes were just lengths of cloth. These could be wrapped round their bodies to make skirts, **loin cloths** or cloaks. Cloaks were very important. The **embroidery** on them showed what their owner did. Aztecs who were brave in battle had special cloaks. A warrior who captured two prisoners was given a cloak with an orange border. Cloaks were given as tributes and were used for trading.

Learning to weave
This glyph from a codex shows a mother teaching her daughter to weave. We have to rely on glyphs like these to tell us what Aztecs wore because all the cloth and clothes have now rotted away.

13

Family life

When a man and a woman got married, the calpulli gave them a plot of land. They grew food on this land. When they had children and needed to grow more food, they asked the calpullec for more land. If a family did not farm the land properly, the capullec took it away from them and gave it to another family who needed it. Every family had to do some work for the capullec and give him some of their crops.

An Aztec wedding
This picture of an Aztec wedding was drawn by Aztecs. The bride and groom are sitting together on a mat at the top of the picture. Their cloaks are tied together. This shows that they are now tied together as husband and wife.

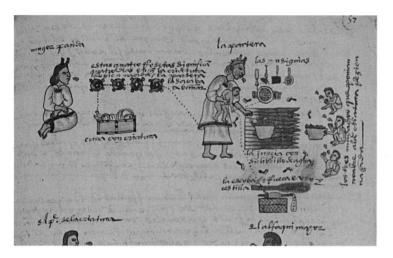

The first days in a baby's life
On the left of the picture a mother is talking to her baby. We know that the baby is four days old because there are four rosettes above the cradle. The midwife, who helped when the baby was born, is in the middle of the picture. She is taking the baby to be washed.

Marriage

Aztec parents arranged the marriages of their children. When a boy was about twenty years old, his father organized a feast and found a suitable girl for him to marry. A **matchmaker** sorted out the details of the **dowry**. This was a present of land or goods from the bride's father to her new husband. A priest advised on the best date for the wedding.

Babies

As soon as a baby was born, the parents went to see a priest. The priest told them what sort of life the baby would have, and chose a lucky day on which to name the baby.

Children's Toys

Aztec boys played with tiny bows and arrows, shields and spears. They played with small tools of their father's craft or trade. Aztec girls played with tiny spindles for spinning thread, brooms and cooking pots. These toys helped boys and girls to learn the sorts of things they would need to know about when they were grown up.

Growing up and going to school

At home children learned the sorts of things they would need to do when they were grown up. Boys helped their fathers farm and fish. Girls helped their mothers spin and weave, cook and clean.

Boys' schools

Boys had to go to school. Most boys went to a **telpocticalli**. This was a school run by their calpulli. They learned how to fight and how to farm. Boys from noble families went to a temple school, the **calmecac.** They learned how to become judges and generals, priests and government officials.

Aztec parents teaching young children
The fathers are on the left of the picture. They are teaching their sons. One son is three years old and the other one is four. How do we know this? The mothers on the right of the picture are teaching their daughters.

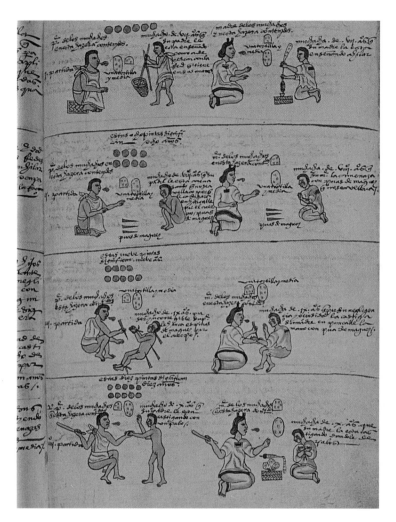

Parents teaching and punishing older children

In the top pictures a father is teaching his son to fish and a mother is teaching her daughter to spin. In the other pictures fathers are punishing their sons and mothers are punishing their daughters. Aztec parents were very strict.

Girls' schools

Girls didn't have to go to school. The daughters of nobles could go to a calmecac if their parents wanted them to. If they did, they learned how to be **priestesses** and healers. They spent a lot of time in silence.

What did the Aztecs believe?

Aztecs worshipped many different gods. They believed that the gods controlled everything in their lives and everything that grew on the Earth. It was therefore important that they kept the gods happy. The Aztecs did this by having religious ceremonies for almost everything that happened in their lives.

Life after death

The Aztecs believed that people lived on when their life on this Earth was over. The kind of afterlife they had depended on the way they had lived in this life. For example, a brave soldier would travel round the earth for four years and then return to Earth as a hummingbird. A woman who died in childbirth would become a goddess. When someone died, their family dressed them in their best clothes. The family danced and chanted funeral prayers for four days. Then the dead Aztec's body was **cremated**. The ashes were buried with the Aztec's possessions and enough food for the long journey to the **underworld** and a new life.

Household gods
Every home had statues of the gods that were specially worshipped by the family that lived there.

THE AZTEC GODS

The Aztecs believed that the gods lived above the Earth. They thought the gods lived in thirteen layers of heaven. The most powerful gods lived in the very top layer.

The most important god was called Huitzilpochtli. He was the Sun God and the God of War. Aztecs believed that if they didn't please Huitzilpochtli the sun would go out and the world would be in darkness. This is why they had to worship him. They did this by killing people and offering their blood to the sun. Aztecs believed the sun needed human blood to give it strength and keep it moving across the sky.

Quetzalcoatl was the god who looked after learning and schools. He was also the God of the Wind who made new life.

Chalchihuitlicue was the Water Goddess. She was married to Tlaloc, the God of Rain.

A mask of the god Quetzalcoatl
It is decorated with turquoise.

A mask of the goddess Chalchihuitlicue

Ceremonies and temples

Ceremonies

The Aztecs had important religious ceremonies every few weeks. Most of these were to do with the farming year. Aztecs prayed to Tlaloc, the Rain God, and to the goddesses of water, maize and the land.

The Aztecs believed their gods wanted human blood. Without it, they believed the sun would not rise in the morning. Aztec priests **sacrificed** thousands of men, women and children in their **temples**. A priest held a **victim** down, facing upwards, on a special stone. Then another priest cut open the victim's chest. The heart was held up to the sun and then put in a **sacred** dish. Most people were probably glad to die like this. They were sure they would go straight to the highest heaven.

Not all their ceremonies took place every day or even every year. Aztecs believed that one age would end and another begin every 52 years. They made special sacrifices to please the gods, to make sure that a new age did begin.

A carving of a boy with a melon
This boy is offering a melon to the gods. Many boys became priests when they grew up. Priests taught in the schools, organized religious ceremonies, kept the fires burning in the temples and sacrificed to the gods.

Temples

There were many temples in every city. The Aztecs built their temples by first making huge mounds of earth. Then they covered them with mud bricks or stone. They built hundreds of steps into the sides of the pyramids. This was so that the priests, and their sacrifices, could get to the top. At the top of each pyramid the Aztecs built a temple. The temples were high up, to be near to the gods. They were also high up so that everyone could watch what the priests were doing.

The great temple and square in Tenochtitlan
This is a modern drawing. We know the great temple and square in Tenochtitlan probably looked like this. The Spaniards wrote detailed descriptions of what Tenochtitlan looked like. Archaeologists have dug up much of what is left of the city.

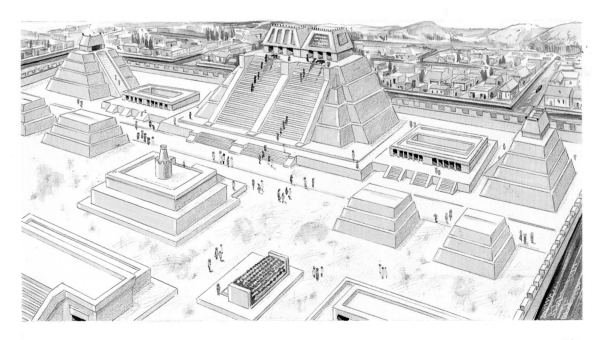

The Aztec calendar

It was important to the Aztecs that they had an accurate calendar. They needed to know when to plant their crops and when to harvest them. They needed to know when to hold their religious ceremonies. They needed to know which days were lucky and which were unlucky. The Aztecs had two calendars. One, the Sun calendar, was very much like ours. Aztecs used it to work out the seasons of the year. The other, the Sacred calendar, was important for the priests and **astrologers**.

The Aztec Sun calendar
This Calendar Stone was carved by the Aztecs in the 1470s. When the Spaniards came, the stone was lost for 200 years. Then it was dug up by accident in 1790. The Sun God is in the middle of the stone.

A carving showing the 'tying up of the years'
The Aztecs believed that every 52 years one age ended and a new age began. The priests kept count by saving a reed each year. When they had a bundle of 52, they tied them together and buried them. A new age was beginning.

The Sun calendar

Aztecs called this calendar the **haab**. It divided the year into eighteen months and each month into twenty days. Because a year is 365 days long, this left five days over. Aztecs said that these five days were very unlucky. No one did anything important then. Babies born then would come to a bad end.

The Sacred calendar

Aztecs called this calendar the **tonalpohualli**. This means the 'Count of Days'. The tonalpohualli divided the year into 260 days. Each day in the year had a different meaning. Priests and astrologers used this calendar for telling what would happen in the future and for deciding which days were lucky and which were unlucky.

The Count of Days
Each day from 1 to 20 had a glyph to describe it. These are some of them.

The city of Tenochtitlan

The Aztecs built their first temple on an island in the middle of a swampy lake. A city grew up around this temple. The Aztecs called this city Tenochtitlan, which means 'The Place of the Fruit of the Prickly Pear Cactus'.

Building the city

The Aztecs were very good **engineers**. They built three **causeways** over the swamp to link the city with the mainland. There were bridges in the causeways which could be taken down to leave gaps and stop enemies entering the city. The engineers built stone **aqueducts** which brought fresh water from the mainland to the city.

Inside the city

By 1519 about 200 000 people lived in Tenochtitlan. The houses were one storey high and had flat roofs. In the middle of the city was a large square. In the square was the emperor's palace and the great temple. There were not many roads. People travelled in **canoes** along the **canals** which linked all parts of the city.

A plan of Tenochtitlan
This plan was drawn by Cortes when the Spaniards invaded. You can see the main square in the middle with the temple on one side of it.

The lake city of Tenochtitlan
This is a modern drawing of Tenochtitlan. How do you think the artist knew what to draw?

Floating gardens

Tenochtitlan stood on an island in the middle of the swampy Lake Texcoco. Lake Texcoco was linked to four other shallow, swampy lakes. The land around them was dry because there was very little rain.

The Aztecs drained parts of Lake Texcoco. On the drained land they made thousands of swamp gardens, called **chinampas**. The gardens were linked by drainage ditches. These were used to **irrigate** the gardens.

The maguey cactus plant
This is a modern photograph of the maguey cactus plant. Aztecs used nearly every part of it. They used its spines as needles and for pricking children when they were naughty. They spun cactus fibres together to make thread which they wove into cloth. The pulp was made into a drink called pulque and used as medicine.

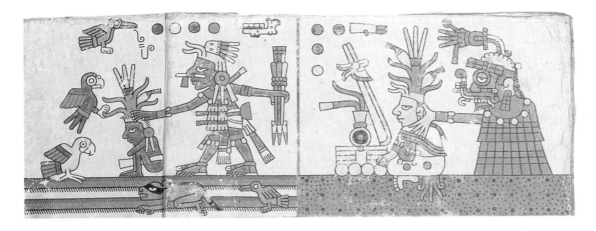

The life of a maize plant

Maize was so important to the Aztecs that special gods and goddesses were in charge of it. On the right of the first picture, Tlaloc the Rain God pours water on the plant. In the second year, on the left, there is no rain. Xipe Totec, the God of Planting and the Spring, is in charge. The soil is hard. The plants cannot take root. They are attacked by birds. In the third year, on the right of the second picture, the Storm Goddess pours water onto a strong, young plant. The fourth year, on the left, is bad again.

Feeding the people

As Tenochtitlan grew, the Aztecs drained more and more land. Farmers had only hoes and digging sticks, but the land was very **fertile** and crops grew easily. The Aztecs grew maize, tomatoes, beans, chilli peppers and prickly pears. They grew maguey cactus. From the cactus they made a drink called **pulque**, and from its fibres they wove cloth. They grew **cocoa** trees, too. Aztecs used cocoa beans for trading and to make a chocolate drink.

27

Aztec homes

There were big differences between the homes of rich Aztecs and the homes of poor Aztecs.

Poor Aztecs lived on the edge of Tenochtitlan. Their houses were made from reeds which were woven together and then plastered with mud. They usually had just one room.

Richer Aztecs, such as craft-workers, lived closer to the centre of Tenochtitlan. Their houses were built from **adobe**, bricks made from mud. They had several rooms which opened onto a central courtyard.

Most ordinary families had a separate, outside bath-house. Many families kept turkeys for meat and eggs and bee-hives for honey.

Nobles lived in the middle of Tenochtitlan. Their palaces were built from beautifully carved stone. Many of them had over a hundred rooms and courtyards which were full of flowers. The grand houses and palaces were whitewashed so that they gleamed in the sun.

The king's palace
This Aztec drawing gives us some idea of what Montezuma's palace looked like. It was almost like a small town. You can see the emperor Montezuma on the top floor in the middle of the picture. This was where he lived. On the ground floor there were council offices, law courts and store rooms for tributes.

Inside an Aztec home

Aztecs did not have much furniture. Everyone slept on woven mats which were spread on the floor at night. During the day they sat on large cushions filled with straw. Families had cooking pots and storage jars made from clay, as well as grinding stones for grinding maize into flour. Every home had a special **shrine** for their household god.

Inside an Aztec house
Can you tell whether this is the house of a rich or a poor Aztec family?

A priest's house in Teotihuacan
This is a modern photograph of a house which was built at the same time as the Aztecs built theirs. It is probably very like the houses Aztec nobles lived in.

Cooking and eating

Aztec wives spent their time cooking, weaving and looking after their children. Even the wives of nobles were expected to be good cooks so that they could organize their servants.

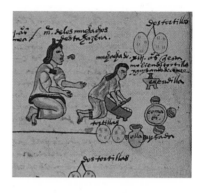

Everyday food

Maize was the Aztecs' main food. The women ground it into flour and made **tortillas**, which were a sort of pancake. They made a porridge from maize. This was called **atolli**. Sometimes they added honey or chillies to the atolli.

Aztecs ate a lot of beans. The women usually boiled them and flavoured them with tomato and chilli. They gathered wild fruit and vegetables, such as figs and nuts, to add to their meals.

Grinding maize
In the top picture a mother is teaching her daughter how to grind maize to make flour. The girl is using a roller made of stone, called a **metate**, to crush the grains. The metate was rolled up and down a block of stone called a **mano**.
In the bottom picture Aztecs are storing grain in pots. Pots like these are still used in Mexico today.

Turkeys and dogs were the only animals the Aztecs kept to eat. They had to hunt for any other meat they wanted. Aztecs trapped rabbits and deer, and netted the wild ducks that flew over the lakes. They fished in the lakes for turtles, newts, salamanders, frogs, tadpoles and shellfish.

Pottery bowls
These bowls were used for preparing food. There are scratch marks on the insides of them. This means they were probably used for grinding peppers. Aztecs made these bowls by coiling strips of clay. They did not have potters' wheels. There were no knives and forks. Everyone ate with their fingers.

Special food
On special occasions ordinary Aztecs might roast a duck or a turkey, a rabbit or a puppy. Rich Aztecs ate this sort of food all the time. They often ate roast pheasants and wild pigs. When they had special feasts they ate roast quail, pigeons, geese, pelicans and cranes. Most people drank pulque. However, the nobles' favourite drink was **chocolatl**. Aztecs made this from cocoa beans. They crushed the beans and made a frothy drink flavoured with **vanilla** and spices.

A hairless dog
This is a pottery model of an Aztec hairless dog. Aztecs kept them to roast and to eat.

Feasts and fun

The rich nobles in Tenochtitlan often held large feasts. Their houses were scented with perfumes of herbs and flowers. Their servants served food to the guests. The guests ate with their fingers, but washed their hands before and after the feast. They smoked tobacco in pipes or cigars. They crushed dried tobacco leaves to make **snuff**.
Women went to these banquets, but no one knows whether they smoked.

Food for the Emperor

When the Emperor Montezuma had a feast there were over a hundred different sorts of food for the guests to choose from. There were roast meats of all kinds in different sauces, with every sort of different vegetables and fruit. The cooks made sweet pastries from maize flour and sugar.

The tables were decorated with gold and silver vases. Cups and spoons were made from gold, silver and tortoiseshell. The spoons were just for serving. Everyone ate with their fingers.

The Aztecs were good dancers.
This pottery model is of a trained dancer and singer. You can see he is wearing a loin cloth which he is holding with one hand. He also has a lip plug and earrings.

32

Music and dancing

After feasts, the Aztecs danced. Orchestras played drums, rattles, flutes, whistles and trumpets made from shell.

Ceremonies and festivals for the gods always included singing and dancing. Every temple had a **tlapizcatzin**, who trained singers. Singers and dancers were very important to the Aztecs.

An Aztec drum
The outside of this drum is made of carved wood. On top are two flaps of wood which made different musical notes when the drummer hit them. The Aztecs called this kind of two-tone drum a teponaztli.

A pottery whistle
Musicians played small whistles like this. They also played pottery flutes and rattles made from hollowed out gourds.

Sports and games

Games

Aztec nobles played a game called **tlachtli**. They played it at special times, such as religious festivals. Two teams played on a stone court surrounded by stone walls. To score, one team had to get a small rubber ball through a stone ring set high in the wall. The players were only allowed to touch the ball with their knees, elbows or hips. Players were often hurt and sometimes killed. Everyone came to watch and cheer for their team.

A tlachtli court
This is a modern photograph of a tlachtli court at Chichen Itza. Mayans, Toltecs and Aztecs played tlachtli. They played it with a ball made from the sap of rubber trees. They grow wild in the rain forests of South America.

Gambling

All Aztecs played a game called **patolli**. They had to throw a dice and move coloured beans on a board until they got three beans in a row. Aztecs held patolli competitions where gamblers bet heavily. Some Aztecs lost all that they had. One Spanish writer tells how people gambled their homes, their fields, their corn granaries and their cactus plants – and lost. They and their families had to become slaves.

The volador ceremony
This is a photograph of a volador ceremony which is held in Mexico today. It is very like the Aztec ceremony. Aztecs tried to copy the way the gods flew through the skies.

63.

A patolli game
We know about patolli from Aztec pictures like this and from Spanish writers. A Spanish writer called Duran tells us that keen players carried their own game mats around with them. They also carried their own dice tied up in small cloths.

Crafts and trades

Many Aztecs were craft-workers. Stone-workers, carpenters, potters, mat and basket workers, and weavers made everyday objects. Luxury objects were made by feather-workers and metal-workers, sculptors, jewellers and painters.

Feather-workers
It took years to learn to be a feather-worker. Parents taught their children all the skills they needed to know. You can see some of them here.
First the pattern was designed. Then the children mixed the glues while the men prepared the cotton backing. The cotton was glued and reglued until it was stiff and shiny. The design was traced on to the cotton. The women prepared the feathers. They came from colourful birds such as quetzals and parrots.

Guilds

Craft-workers lived and worked in separate areas of Aztec cities. They worshipped their own gods. Usually whole families worked at the same craft. Because they lived in the same calpulli they were able to organize themselves into **guilds** and train **apprentices**.

Craft-workers

Aztecs did not use wheels. They did not use carts or pulleys to carry and lift raw materials such as stone, wood and metal. Slaves did this work. Aztecs did not have iron from which to make knives, chisels and other tools. They used blades, made from a mixture of copper and tin, to cut and carve stone and wood. Aztec potters did not use potters' wheels. They made coil pots and then smoothed them until there were no bumps left.

Feather-workers, goldsmiths, silversmiths, jewellers and painters worked only for the nobility. They made gold nose and lip plugs. They used precious stones such as rubies to make necklaces and bracelets.

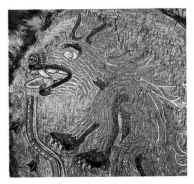

A feather-work shield
This shield was made by feather-workers. All the feathers were glued on to cotton which had been stretched over a wooden frame.

A turquoise ornament
This ornament is made from gold and decorated with a stone called turquoise. A nobleman would have worn this on his chest. Aztec craft-workers made jewellery and other ornaments.

Buying and selling

Every village, town and city in the Aztec Empire had an open-air market. Most markets were open five days a week. People went there to buy and sell. They went there to meet their friends.

Bartering

Aztecs did not use money. They bought and sold goods by **barter**. They swapped what they had to sell for goods which were worth the same. The value of goods was carefully worked out. Everything, whether gold, maize or a slave, could be valued in cocoa beans or cotton cloaks, called **quachtli**.

The market at Tenochtitlan

Every day a great market was held in the centre of Tenochtitlan. Thousands of people came from all over the Aztec Empire to buy and sell goods. They brought luxuries such as golden goblets and jade necklaces; they brought ordinary things such as black beans and pottery dishes; they brought slaves and puppies and salt. Officials made sure that the buyers and sellers did not cheat or charge prices that were too high.

The market at Tenochtitlan

This is a modern reconstruction of the Aztec market at Tenochtitlan. The sellers spread out what they had to sell on mats. They sat on the ground and waited for buyers. Vegetables were sold in one part of the market, pottery in another, and so on. There were no shops so people had to buy everything they needed in the markets.

Aztec prices
The Aztecs measured the price of something by how many cloaks (quachtli) or how many cocoa beans it was worth.
Here are some examples:
1 dug-out canoe = 1 cloak
1 slave = 25 cloaks
1 feather cape = 100 cloaks

Aztec merchants

Merchants (called **pochteca** by the Aztecs) travelled all over the Aztec Empire and far beyond it. They looked for goods to buy and bring back to the cities. They looked for gold and silver, copper and precious stones for the craft-workers. The craft-workers depended on the merchants for the materials they needed. The merchants took with them luxury goods such as gold necklaces, ruby earrings and **obsidian** razors to sell far and wide. Merchants travelled in groups with porters to carry the heavy stuff. They only travelled on specially lucky days. They kept their trading details secret. They returned to their cities at night and hid their goods immediately.

Aztec merchants
These pictures are from an Aztec codex. The merchant is in the right-hand picture. He is carrying quetzal feathers on his back. Merchants had their own god, Yacatecuhtli. He is in the left-hand picture. He is carrying a cross-roads sign on his back. A footprint was the Aztec glyph for a journey. Can you find the footprints in this picture?

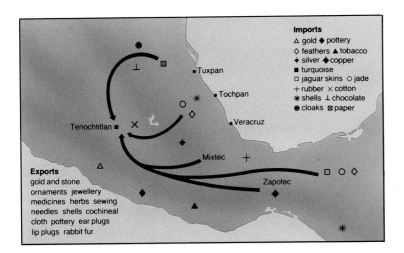

Imports
△ gold ◆ pottery
◇ feathers ▲ tobacco
✦ silver ◆ copper
■ turquoise
▢ jaguar skins ○ jade
+ rubber × cotton
✳ shells ⊥ chocolate
● cloaks ⊠ paper

Exports
gold and stone
ornaments jewellery
medicines herbs sewing
needles shells cochineal
cloth pottery ear plugs
lip plugs rabbit fur

Aztec trading
This map shows where the Aztecs traded and the goods they bought and sold.

Merchant guilds

Merchants were important people. They had their own guild and their own law courts. They could own land. They were allowed to send their children to the calmecac with the nobles' children. The government was in charge of all trading and shared in the profits from the goods the merchants brought back.

Merchant spies

Merchants travelled far and wide. Some of them brought back information for the emperor. They told him about plots in far-away towns. They told him about strangers who had arrived in the Aztec Empire.

Travel and transport

The Aztecs never discovered that wheels could be used to move things about, so they did not have carts and wagons.

There were no horses, donkeys or oxen in the whole of the Aztec Empire. This meant that the Aztecs could not use animals as pack animals to carry their goods. Everything that had to be carried over land was carried on the backs of porters, who were sometimes slaves.

Difficult journeys

Some overland journeys were very difficult. They were made by merchants who travelled across mountain ranges, through steaming jungles and over burning sandy plains. They travelled in groups called **caravans**. Sometimes soldiers went with them to guard them. Merchants and soldiers were the only Aztecs who travelled really long distances. Nobles travelled between Tenochtitlan and their lands in the country, but these journeys were not long ones.

Merchants carrying weapons
These Aztec pictures tell us that Aztec merchants carried weapons when they travelled. Why do you think they needed to do this?

The volcano of Popacatapetl

This photograph of the volcano Popacatapetl gives us an idea of what the Aztec countryside looked like. It must have been difficult for merchants to make long journeys on foot over land like this.

Canals and waterways

Most Aztecs used flat bottomed wooden boats and canoes to travel around Technotitlan and out to their fields.

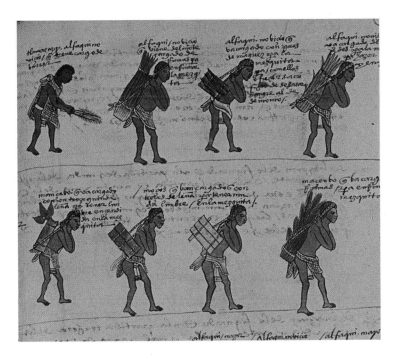

Aztec porters

These Aztec pictures show porters carrying trading goods for the merchants. Each porter carried between 20 kg and 30 kg on his back. Can you see the strap going round their foreheads? How would this make it easier to carry heavy goods?

Early history

Most of the Aztecs' early history is based on legends. One legend says that long ago they left an island home called Aztlan. This was because their priests told them that the god Huitzilopochtli would make them lords of the world.

The Aztecs' wanderings
The Aztecs would have wandered through countryside like this on their journey from Aztlan to the Valley of Mexico.

The Hill of the Locust

The Valley of Mexico was already divided into **city-states** when the Aztecs arrived. The Aztecs tried to take over some farmland, but the other tribes drove them away. In 1299 they arrived at Chapultepec, 'The Hill of the Locust'. The Aztecs settled down and began to farm. However, within twenty years the other tribes had driven them out to the shores of Lake Texcoco.

Tenochtitlan

The Aztecs fled to Culhuacan on the other side of the Lake. The Culhua people forced them to live on dry and barren land, hoping they would die there. The Aztecs, however, did well and soon wanted more land. They had to fight the Culhua for this. Eventually the Aztecs fled to an island in the middle of Lake Texcoco. On the island the Aztecs found a cactus with an eagle perched on it, carrying a snake in its beak. This is what the god Huitzilopochtli had told them to look for. They knew they had to build a city there and settle down. Huitzilpochtli would then make them lords of the world.

The Aztecs settle
This is a picture from an Aztec codex. It shows the beginnings of Tenochtitlan. In the middle is the cactus with the eagle perched on the top. Can you find the lake and the four quarters of the city the Aztecs were going to build?

Building an empire

The first Aztec ruler in Tenochtitlan was Tenoc. He made peace with the Culhua people. A Culhua called Acamapichtli became the next ruler of the Aztecs. The **alliance** with the Culhua gave the Aztecs more power. However, the Tepaneca tribe were still the most powerful in the valley. They seized city-states and began to build an empire. The Aztecs quickly made an alliance with them.

The Aztecs gain power

In 1426 the Aztecs had a new leader, Itzcoatl. Under him, the Aztecs allied with the people in the cities of Texcoco and Tlacoan. Together, in 1428, they defeated the Tepaneca and captured their capital city.

The Aztec Empire grows

Itzcoatl died in 1440. His nephew, Montezuma I, became **emperor**. Montezuma wanted to make the Aztec Empire bigger by conquering lands outside the valley. He had bad luck.

The Aztec rulers

Ruler	Reign
Acamapichtli	(1372–1391)
Huitzilhuitl	(1391–1415)
Chimalpopoca	(1415–1426)
Itzcoatl	(1426–1440)
Montezuma I	(1440–1468)
Axayacatl	(1468–1481)
Tizoc	(1481–1486)
Ahuitzotl	(1486–1502)
Montezuma II	(1502–1520)

Itzcoatl

Ahuitzotl

Montezuma II

The Stone of Tizoc
This is a carving showing the great deeds of Tizoc, an Aztec king. Can you see him holding on to the hair of a prisoner?

In 1446 Tenochtitlan was badly flooded. Then there were years of bad harvests and famine. Thousands of Aztecs died. Montezuma was determined that this would not happen again. He set out to conquer wealthy lands where there was good farmland. The Aztecs did not settle on these conquered lands. They let the lords stay in control so long as they paid tributes to the Aztecs.

The Aztec Empire was large and powerful when Montezuma died in 1468. In 1502, when the ruler Ahuitzotl died, the nobles chose his nephew, Montezuma II to rule. He was to make the Aztec Empire even greater.

Aztec warriors

The Aztecs were ruthless warriors. They built up an empire because of their skill at fighting.

A successful warrior

Most boys wanted to be warriors. Young boys were trained to fight. They were taught how to take prisoners. When a boy was ten years old his hair was cut, leaving a lock of hair at the back of his neck. This lock was cut off when the boy took his first prisoner. When he had captured or killed four prisoners, he was allowed to wear a special **cape** and join in battle discussions. After that, he could become a **tlacateccatl** or commander.

Dressing for battle
War lords and knights wore splendid uniforms covered with feather-work. The type and colour of the feathers showed a soldier's rank. For example, a captain always wore red feathers.

The Aztec army

The Aztecs had an army of full-time professional soldiers. The best fighters became eagle knights who wore eagle's head helmets in battle, or jaguar knights who wore jaguar skins in battle. Under them came thousands of ordinary warriors.

All Aztec men, except slaves, had to do military service and learn how to fight. When there was a war all the calpullis had to send as many men as possible to fight. They were organized into companies of 200 to 400 men. The companies were grouped into larger regiments. Every regiment was commanded by a professional soldier.

Aztec warriors fought with spears and **javelins** that could be thrown a long way. Some Aztecs fought with wooden sticks edged with sharpened obsidian. They wore armour made of cotton which was padded to make it thicker and then soaked in salt water. This made the cotton stiff so that it could not be pierced so easily. Warriors carried shields covered in hide and decorated with feathers.

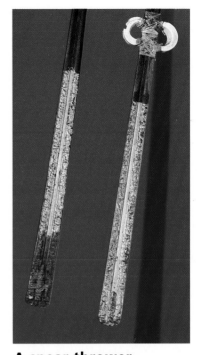

A spear thrower
Warriors hurled spears and javelins with these spear throwers. The spear slotted into a groove and was held by a hook. A warrior could throw a spear at great speed using one of these spear throwers. The Aztecs called a spear thrower an atlatl.

Aztec warfare

Aztec rulers would start a fight for almost any reason – maybe someone had insulted them, or a city had not paid its tribute.

Planning the attack

Aztecs did not launch surprise attacks. First they sent nobles to the city they planned to attack. The nobles asked the city's leader to join the Aztecs. The city had twenty days in which to decide. Aztec nobles would visit the city twice more, and each time they threatened and warned. If, finally, the city would not agree to pay tribute to the Aztecs, war was declared. The Aztecs, meanwhile, had had plenty of time to spy out the land!

Huitzilopochtli, the Sun God and the God of War
Aztecs took as many prisoners as possible so that they could sacrifice them to Huitzilopochtli. They took the prisoners away in long lines, with their hands tied behind them and their necks in wooden collars.

A prisoner
This prisoner is being threatened by four jaguar knights. If he defeated all four knights, the Aztecs would let him live. If not, he would be sacrificed.

Medicine and healing

An Aztec who was ill visited a **diviner.** The diviner threw maize seeds onto a mat. He could tell what the illness was just by looking at the pattern made by the seeds. The ill person then went to see a **ticitl,** who was a doctor. The ticitl knew how to use more than 130 herbs to make different kinds of medicines. They used mushrooms a lot. They gave patients steam baths to sweat a fever out.

Some ticitl went to war with the Aztec armies. They set broken bones and used different mixtures to treat wounds.

These two pictures show the ticitl at work.

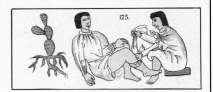

Launching the attack

Aztec leaders then got the army together. Warriors came from all over the Empire to fight the enemy. Priests decided on a lucky day to fight the battle.

The battle was usually short and fierce. Aztecs did not try to kill enemy soldiers. They aimed to take them prisoner so that they could sacrifice them later. If the Aztecs won, they decided on the tribute the defeated city had to pay. Aztecs burned temples and made the defeated people worship the Aztec god Huitzilopochtli.

Montezuma the emperor

Montezuma II became emperor in 1502. Tenochtitlan was a huge city. Most, but not all, of the neighbouring cities were part of the Aztec Empire. The land around them belonged to the Empire. Conquering new lands meant longer and longer journeys. The warriors began to complain.

A new idea
Montezuma decided to try something different. He attacked the nearby city-states that were not part of the Empire.

Montezuma wearing his royal robes
A nobleman is helping Montezuma put on his headdress. Montezuma is wearing nose and ear plugs.

The Ashen bird
Aztecs said that when this bird appeared, something evil was going to happen. In an Aztec story, some fishermen brought this bird to Montezuma. He looked in the mirror on its crest and saw warriors riding on deer.

The Spanish arrive

While the fighting was going on, Montezuma faced new and frightening events.

For several years the Aztecs had received **omens** that something evil was going to happen. Some Aztecs saw tongues of fire in the skies; some saw Lake Texcoco boil; others said that lightening struck a temple and a shrine burst into flames. Then, suddenly, messengers began arriving in Tenochtitlan with strange tales. They said that white skinned men with beards had arrived on the east coast and were travelling through Maya country. They were getting closer and closer to Tenochtitlan. Montezuma remembered an old Aztec legend. The god Quetzalcoatl had long ago vanished across the sea in the east. It was said that one day he would come back and claim his kingdom. The Aztecs were afraid. Were these white men from the east really gods? How could the Aztecs possibly fight a battle with gods? If they were men, what new weapons had they brought with them from across the sea?

Montezuma goes to meet Cortes
This is a Spanish painting. It shows the Aztec emperor, Montezuma, setting out to meet Hernan Cortes, the leader of the Spanish expedition. In what ways does Montezuma look different here to the way he looks in Aztec paintings? Why do you think this is?

The Spanish conquistadores

In 1518 a Spanish captain called Juan de Grijalva led an expedition to the east coast of Mexico. While he was there he met a tax collector called Pinotl, who told him about an inland kingdom which had plenty of gold. Grijalva took this information back to Spain with him. A new expedition was organized. The commander was a soldier and explorer, Hernan Cortes.

The Aztecs meet Cortes

In 1519 Cortes, and his men landed at Veracruz. Quickly Montezuma made plans. He sent priests and warriors to meet the **conquistadores** at Veracruz. They took precious gifts for the men they thought were gods. Cortes challenged them to fight, but they were afraid and fled back to Tenochtitlan. Montezuma was puzzled. He sent more gifts, and watched and waited. Meanwhile, Cortes and his men began to march toward Tenochtitlan. Before they left Veracruz they burnt the boats that had brought them there. There was no going back.

A Spanish portrait of Hernan Cortes
This picture was painted when Cortes was about 34 years old. This was just before he set out on his expedition to Mexico.

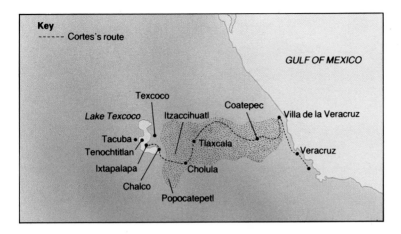

This map shows the route taken by Cortes on his journey to Tenochtitlan in 1519.

Cortes marches to Tenochtitlan

No one really knows what Cortes was like. Some historians say he was a great general. Others say he was cunning and greedy for gold. We do know, however, that his men were ready to follow him through unknown lands and dangers.

Cortes and his army of 400 Spaniards began their march across mountainous countryside. Suddenly, when they reached Tlaxcala, high in the mountains, they were surrounded by thousands of warriors. Cortes had horses and guns which the Tlaxcalans had never seen before. Cortes and his men won the battle. The Tlaxcalans agreed to join forces with Cortes against the Aztecs. Together they marched to Tenochtitlan.

Montezuma's men meet Cortes at Veracruz

Montezuma's men took gifts to Cortes. When they left he fired a gun. The Aztecs were very frightened.

55

The fall of Tenochtitlan

Thousands of Aztecs watched as the conquistadores marched up to Tenochtitlan. Montezuma met them on a causeway outside the city. He welcomed them as if they were gods. He took them to a palace where they were to stay, as honoured guests of the Aztecs.

The Spaniards were amazed when they saw the riches of Tenochtitlan. They decided they had to have it all for themselves. They invited Montezuma to stay with them as a guest in their palace, but they treated him as a prisoner. He did all he could to please the Spaniards. Then Cortes began to complain about the statues of Aztec gods and their human sacrifices. Montezuma was very angry.

The death of Montezuma

Aztec warriors gathered in Tenochtitlan to celebrate the midsummer festival. A Spanish commander, Alvardo, thought they were going to attack the conquistadores. He ordered his men to kill hundreds of Aztecs. The Aztecs fought back. As Montezuma tried to calm them he was killed.

Cortes speaking to Montezuma
Cortes is being helped to understand what Montezuma is saying by Dona Marina. She spoke Nahuatl and Spanish.

The Aztecs imprisoning the Spaniards
The Aztecs at first treated the Spaniards like gods. Then, when Cortes took Montezuma prisoner, the Aztecs realized the Spanish were not to be trusted.

The Spaniards conquer Mexico
This is a Spanish painting. You can see the differences between Spanish and Aztec arms and armour. Do you think this meant that the Spaniards were bound to win in the end?

Victory to the conquistadores

Cortes and his men fought their way out of Tenochtitlan. About 300 of them survived. They then had to face a vast Aztec army at Otumba. The Aztecs tried to capture the Spaniards alive so they could sacrifice them later. The Spaniards concentrated on killing as many Aztecs as possible. The Spaniards won.

Other tribes quickly joined the Spaniards. They wanted to wipe out the hated Aztecs. Together they fought their way back up the causeways into Tenochtitlan. They **blockaded** the city so that no supplies could get in. Thousands of Aztecs died. The Spaniards finally captured the city in April 1521. The Aztec Empire was gone for ever.

New Spain

The Aztecs were defeated because they were fighting an enemy they did not understand. They fought to please the gods and take captives. The Spaniards fought with superior weapons and aimed to kill the Aztec commanders first, so that there was no one to give orders to the ordinary Aztec warriors.

Spanish rule

Ten years after the Conquest, the whole of Mexico was under Spanish rule. It was called New Spain, and Cortes was made governor. Spanish settlers made the Aztecs work for them. In return they converted them to Christianity. The Aztecs became slaves to the Spaniards.

Aztecs at a Christian religious service
After the Spaniards had conquered the Aztecs, Christian missionaries arrived in Mexico. The Spaniards thought they were making things better for the Aztecs by turning them into Christians and by teaching them to read and write, and to work in the European way. In fact they were destroying the Aztecs' way of life.

Thousands of Aztecs died because of the way the Spaniards treated them. They died from accidents, from overwork and from pneumonia. Thousands more died from the European diseases the Spaniards brought with them: smallpox, measles, chicken-pox and typhus.

The legacy of the Aztecs

The Spaniards ruled in New Spain until 1821. The Aztecs were forced to give up their lands and their way of life. Today there are only about 3000 Aztecs in Mexico. They still speak Nahuatl. They still hold some of the Aztec festivals, but these are mainly for the tourists.

The ruins of Montezuma's summer palace
The Spaniards tore down Tenochtitlan. They destroyed everything. They melted down the gold objects. Some things were sent back to Spain and these have survived. The only other artefacts that were not destroyed were buried under the ruins of Tenochtitlan. They are still being found by archaeologists.

The flag of Mexico
The modern flag of Mexico has the Aztec eagle and cactus in the centre.

Time line

BC

1300   Olmec civilization in Mexico

AD

300–900   Maya civilization in Yucatan

900–1150   Toltec empire in Mexico

1111   Aztecs leave Aztlan

1299   Aztecs arrive at Chapultepec

1319   Aztecs flee to Culhuacan

1325   Aztecs build Tenochtitlan

1440   Montezuma I becomes emperor

1502   Montezuma II becomes emperor

1518   Montezuma hears about white men in Mexico

1519   Cortes' fleet lands at Veracruz

1520   Montezuma killed

1521   Fall of Tenochtitlan

1531   Mexico comes under Spanish rule and is called New Spain

1821   End of Spanish rule in Mexico

Pronunciation of Aztec words

Aztec word	Pronunciation
Acamapichtli	A-kama-pich-tlee
calipixque	kal-ip-isk
calpulli	kal-pulee
Chalchinuitlicue	Chal-chi-nooit-licoo
Chicomecoatl/Xilonen	Chiko-me-koatel/Shil-onen
chocolatl	choko-latel
Coatlicue	Koat-likoo
cuicalli	koo-i-kalee
Ehecatl-Quetzalcoatl	E-ekatel/Ket-sal-koatel
Huitzilopochtli	Wit-thil-o-poch-tlee
maguey	mag-oo-ay
Mayahuel	Maya-oo-el
Nahuatl	Na-wa-tel
Ometochtli	Ome-toch-tlee
patolli	pat-olee
pinole	pin-ole
pochteca	poch-teka
Popacatapetl	Popa-kata-petel
pulque	pul-k
quachtli	kach-tlee
Quetzalcoatl	Ket-sal-koatel
telpocticalli	tel-pokti-kale
Tenochtitlan	Ten-och-tit-lan
Teotihuacan	Tai-ot-i-ooa-kan
teponaztli	te-pon-ath-tlee
Tetesinnan	Tet-es-innan
Tezcatlipoca	Teth-kat-li-poka
ticitl	tik-i-tel
tlachtli	tlach-tlee
Tlalacel	Tlal-a-kel
Tlaloc	Tlal-ok
tlapizcatzin	tla-pith-cat-thin
Tlatelolco	Tlat-el-ol-ko
tlatocan	tlat-o-kan
Tochtepec	Toch-te-pek
tonalpohualli	tonal-pok-ooal-ee
tortilla	tort-ee-ya
Xipe Totec	Shipe Totek
Xiuhtecutli	Sheoo-te-kutlee

Glossary

adobe: sun-baked mud bricks

alliance: a union or friendly agreement between two countries or states. They become allies

amatl: a type of paper made from bark

apprentice: a person who learns a craft or a trade by working for a skilled craftsman

aqueduct: a channel made by people for carrying water across a valley

archaeologist: a person who tries to work out what happened in the past by finding and studying old buildings and objects

architect: a person who designs buildings

artefact: an object that was made by people in the past

astrologer: someone who foretells the future by studying the stars

atolli: a type of maize porridge eaten by the Aztecs

barter: to trade or bargain with goods

blockade: to surround a place so that the people are trapped inside with the aim of starving them or forcing them to give in

calmecac: an Aztec temple school for the sons of nobles

calpulli: an organized group of Aztec families who owned land that was farmed by the people. Each calpulli was run by a calpullec or headman

canal: a man-made river

canoe: a long, narrow open boat which is paddled along

cape: a piece of cloth worn round the shoulders, like a short cloak

caravan: a group of merchants travelling together for safety

causeway: a raised roadway across water

chinampa: an Aztec floating garden

chocolatl: an Aztec word for a drink made from cocoa beans

city-state: a city that is also an independent state with its own rulers

civilization: a large group of people who have settled in one place and live in the same organized way. They follow the same customs and produce their own style in art

cocoa: a powder made from the seeds of the cacao tree that grows wild in Central America

codex: an Aztec book of picture symbols. The plural of codex is codices

commoner: a person who is not a noble

conquistadores: Spanish conquerors

council: a group of people who are in charge of the day-to-day organization of a town or city

cotton: fabric woven from the

cremate: to burn a dead body

cuicalli: a school where Aztec children learned religious songs, dances and music

diviner: a person who claims to be able to see the future by using magic

dowry: money given by a bride's father to a bridegroom on their marriage

embroidery: making pictures or patterns on cloth, with coloured threads

empire: a group of countries or states ruled by one king or queen, who may be called an emperor or empress

engineer: someone who designs and build large buildings, bridges etc.

excavate: to dig up buried objects, carefully, to find information about the past

fertile: describes rich soil where plants grow well

glyph: a picture symbol standing for a word or idea

guild: a society of people in the same trade

haab: the Aztec Sun calendar

irrigate: to water crops by channelling water from a river or lake along pipes or ditches

javelin: a type of spear, usually thrown

legend: a well-known story about the past, that is not always true

loin cloth: a cloth that covers the loins, the part of the body between the waist and thighs

maguey: a type of cactus plant

matchmaker: someone who settled the marriage details between two people

mano: block of stone on which grain was laid, to be crushed with a metate

merchant: a person who buys goods in one place and sells them somewhere else, often in a different country

metate: a roller made of stone, used to crush grain

noble: a person of high birth, such as a lord. The group of nobles in one country is called the nobility

obsidian: a dark shiny type of rock which comes from volcanoes

omen: an unusual happening or sign that some people believe means something is about to take place

patolli: a gambling dice game

pochteca: merchant

priest: a man who carries out all the duties and ceremonies for worshipping the gods

priestess: female priest

pulque: a drink made from maguey cactus

quachtli: a cotton cloak worn by Aztecs

sacred: holy, used only in special ceremonies for the gods

sacrifice: to kill an animal or person as an offering to the gods

scribe: a person who wrote out documents and books by hand

sculptor: an artist who makes statues or other objects from stone or metals

shrine: an altar or small chapel to a god or saint

slave: a person who is owned by a master and has to work without pay

snuff: a kind of tobacco that is not smoked, but sniffed through the nose

telpocticalli: a school for the sons of Aztec commoners

temple: building or place where people worshipped the gods

ticitl: an Aztec doctor

tlacateccatl: commander of Aztec warriors

tlachtli: a ball game played in ancient Mexico

tlapizcatzin: the caretaker of an Aztec temple

tlatocan: large council which advised the Aztec king

tonalpohualli: the Aztec Sacred calendar

tortilla: a flat bread made from maize flour

tribute: a type of tax paid in food and other goods

underworld: the place where the Aztecs believed people went when they died. The Aztec underworld had nine layers, ruled over by gods

vanilla: a type of orchid plant. The fruit of the plant is used for flavouring food

victim: person who is sacrificed

warrior: a fighting man, or soldier

Index